Creating Kata

Creating Kata

By: David H. Nielsen

©2008 All rights reserved

Published by LuLu publishers

ISBN 978-0-557-02700-2

Cover Design and Art Work by:

Michael "Miko" Walker

©2008 by David H. Nielsen

All rights reserved

First edition, 2008

Please send any comments to:

www.usatka.com

WARNING

All methods described in this book can be, and are, extremely dangerous when done without the supervision of a qualified martial arts instructor. Any one who attempts to do the methods described in this book does so at their own risk. All methods contained within this book are solely for the information of its readers in order to understand a certain viewpoint of the author. The author cannot and will not be held responsible for any injury incurred by anyone from using the methods discussed in this book. Again, the reader should seek instruction from a qualified martial arts instructor and be examined by a doctor before attempting any methods discussed in this book.

Acknowledgements

There are so many people to thank that I'm not sure where to begin. I guess this is a good problem to have if you are surrounded by some of not only the best and most knowledgeable in the business, but also good friends.

I'll start with Iain Abernethy, who is most definitely responsible for getting me published for the very first time in Traditional Karate magazine. You saw something in my writing that led you to help, like you do for so many others. Mostly, you've remained a friend through my long periods of study, illness, and the like. Thank you from the deepest part of my heart mate.

To all the students that have remained to help form Nahashu Ryu Karate Do. You black belts are extremely loyal and dedicated to me. The future of this system is yours; especially, Michael "Miko" Walker, my assistant, my training partner, and everything else that a guy could want in a friend. You've learned well "Big Mike", the ball will be passed soon enough.

Finally, to all who taught me the art of karate; I could never repay you, except to pass it on. I can assure you that I will do just that.

Dedication

To all my family who stuck by me (you know who you are).

I could not have done this without the support of my friends, who are too numerous to mention. A man is very lucky if he has but one friend in life. I have lots. God bless all of you.

Finally, I must make this special dedication to my wife. Amy, you have given me a new life, new inspiration, and another beautiful daughter. No one has ever supported or stuck by me like you have. You've shown me what true love is and have become one with me in this journey here on earth, until we reach our Father God in our heavenly home. I love you with all my heart. I remain forever, your sailor.

There's no doubt that creating kata is a controversial subject. We traditional karateka tend to, quite rightly, hold the kata passed down to us in very high regard. The traditional kata are the work of the great masters of the past and when people decide to create kata in the modern day it is sometimes difficult to avoid the assumption that they are getting above their station and being arrogant by assuming themselves to be the equal of the founding fathers of our art.

Further controversy is created by the rise of "creative kata" over the last few decades. The traditionalist will see martial artists in brightly coloured gi demonstrate a flamboyant "kata" that they have created for tournaments and then either tut, giggle or weep.

I think it's important for all martial artists to find their own path. Although creative kata is certainly not my thing, I am not aggressively opposed to it. Indeed, I have some admiration for the athleticism displayed during the performances of such kata. The point is that, for the traditionalist, kata is a living record of a brutal combat system. Back flips, cartwheels and movements robbed from dancing, all performed to Survivor's "eye of the tiger", don't really sit well with the brutality at the heart of traditional kata! When people talk of creating kata it is often flamboyant creative kata that the traditionalist envisages and this further adds to the controversy of creating kata within traditional circles.

The other issue that is almost certain to come up during any talk on creating kata is the question of "what's wrong with the kata we already have?". Creating a kata can be seen as inferring that the traditional kata are somehow lacking. The counter argument to this is, of course, the fact that a great many traditional kata were passed down to us. The past masters obviously felt each kata had its own inherent value otherwise there would just be one "mono-kata" throughout karate as a whole. The past masters were taught existing kata, but they also created kata of their own. When looking at creating kata today, it is helpful if we have an understanding of why the masters of old created kata themselves.

Essentially the past masters created kata to encapsulate what they considered to be important combative concepts and principles. The idea was to ensure that these lessons would not be lost and would be passed on to subsequent generations. A good example of this is the tale of the origins of Chinto kata. Chinto kata is named after a Chinese martial artist and sailor. During the 1800s, Chinto became shipwrecked on Okinawa and finding himself stranded without resources he began to steal food and livestock under the cover of night. This was reported to the Okinawan king who sent Sokon Matsumura – his chief bodyguard and a karate master – to deal with the situation. When Matsumura confronted Chinto, he fought back with exceptional skill and Matsumura found himself equally matched; which was a very rare occurrence! Always keen to further his martial skills, Matsumura made a deal with Chinto: he would take care of him in exchange for instruction in Chinto's fighting methods. Matsumura subsequently formulated a kata – named after the originator of the combative methods it contained – to ensure Chinto's methods were recorded and passed on to future generations. Other kata were also developed by an individual's students in order to record what they had been taught. Kata, in the traditional sense, can therefore be defined as *"a record and summary of the key combative techniques and principles of a fighting style or an individual."*

To say we are "traditional martial artists" simply means we are essentially following in the footsteps of the past masters. The past masters innovated, changed things, explored the totality of combat and brought together many sources of information; and then they created kata to encapsulate the essence of a given methodology. Therefore, those who create kata can most certainly be seen as being "traditional"; providing certain requirements are met.

The past masters did not create kata to "look cool" or to indulge their egos. They created kata because they wished to preserve tried and tested combative methods. These were combative methods that they wholeheartedly believed in and that they felt were not specifically addressed in the kata they already knew. These new kata were then passed on to the next generation who – in keeping with our tradition – subjected the kata to their own critical analysis. Following such analysis, and the passing of time, the kata would be passed on unchanged, modified or perhaps even abandoned.

There is no reason at all why the experienced martial artists of today could not create kata – just as the past masters did – to record a combative methodology they consider to be of value. The question is whether the kata truly has value or not? I'm reminded of the oft recited phrase that everyone has at least one book in them … but not necessarily a good one! The same can definitely be said of kata. Just because we can create one, does not mean it is the equal of the kata we have inherited from the past.

One of the things that the traditional kata have going for them is that they have been through the process described above many times. "Martial evolution" and the fact the traditional kata are still with us tells us a great deal about their inherent value. The traditional kata have been deemed valuable by many generations and hence their value has been strongly established.

A kata created today may be passed on for generations and hence become the equal of the traditional ones. Or it may be deemed of little value, abandoned and lost to history; as I'm sure plenty of other kata have been. The determining factor will be whether subsequent generations view the kata as having value. The point is that it that the individual creating the kata has no say in whether their kata is the equal of the kata created by the past masters. That's for history to decide.

Creating a kata does therefore not automatically mean those doing so are assuming themselves to be the equal of the founding fathers of our art. If they believe they have something of value to record, the traditional thing to do is to create a kata to do just that. They should then do as the past masters did and surrender the kata to history for it to decide the kata's value.

Instantly assuming a modern kata is the equivalent of a "time tested" one is certainly an arrogant assumption. However, there is nothing inherently wrong with the creation of kata in itself. Indeed it can be convincingly argued that experienced modern karateka have a duty to create kata for the benefit of future generations. After all, it would have been a great loss to modern karate if Matsumura had not decided to record Chinto's methodology. All the kata we have today are with us because someone created them. Despite the controversy that surrounds the creation of kata, this process of creation is traditional and can be of great value if done by the right people and in the right way.

In this book Dave Nielsen has grabbed the bull by the horns and taken on the controversial subject of kata creation. He's a brave man, as this book is sure to attract plenty of criticism. So what! This is an issue that should be explored and I applaud Dave for pondering this subject and for having the courage to put his head above the parapet and share his thoughts. There's no "this would be a cool place for a summersault!" in this book. Dave has looked at creating kata from a purely traditional perspective and I'm not aware of any other book that has attempted to do that.

Before I conclude this foreword and hand you over to Dave, I'd like to mention one final thing. The vast majority of people reading this book will not have reached the level of experience to create a kata in line with the traditional criteria for doing so. However, even if you don't have the knowledge to create a potentially valuable kata, or you do not have a specific methodology to record, or you don't think what you have to offer will be of benefit to future generations; there could still be benefit in trying to create a kata. Even if the kata proves to have no value to anyone else. Simply going through the creation process may further your understanding of the traditional time tested kata that have been passed on to you. You may also have fun along the way! "Fun" is a good enough reason to do anything and yet it's oft neglected in the thought process of many martial artists. So have fun and enjoy this book!

Iain Abernethy 5th Dan.

FOREWORD

When I first began reading *Creating Kata*, I wasn't quite sure what to think of it. I saw, time and again, things I had been learning since day one of my training with Soke Nielsen. I saw lessons in applying martial arts, but I had never equated them to the idea of forging a Kata. Only as I finished it, all the while remembering events described herein, the essence of the text hit me.

Some may think this book I heresy to the spirit of traditional martial arts. Each have their right to that thought, but I for one will heartily disagree. I have known Soke Nielsen for many years now, and I am here to tell you he is not some Sport Karate flub that thinks Kata are just meaningless dances. I can assure you, this text says nothing of timing one's Kata to music, or changing parts so that it looks better in your Elvis costume. No glowing chrome 'chucks of impending doom. This is a text borne of the masters of the past.

Soke Nielsen is not a man that thinks himself above the masters of the past, like Miyagi Chojun, or Mabuni Kenwa. As long as I have known him, he has been inspired by these masters. He does everything he can to walk his path by their example. He is humble in this quest for his perfection of self, and passes that onto his students: both through how he teaches and how he lives.

I am biased in that much of what is discussed in this text, I have been having drilled into me since my kyu level days. I am one of he lucky ones, being exposed to the sort of insight found in Soke Nielsen for so many years now. It was only after sharing my training experiences with those of other martial traditions that I ever found out my training was unique. These teachings have helped me to find a greater understanding of Kata, Bunkai, and all of Karate.

Creating Kata is the culmination of years of training, research, and sweat. I am proud to even be mentioned in this work, let alone having been a part of the process. From the eyes of one who has seen this text put into action, I can tell you, it works! Do not be fooled by the apparent simplicity of this blueprint. It does not deal with all the martial "hocus pocus" found in some books about the understanding of Kata. There is no mention of Shinto or Buddhism to obscure the essence of Kata behind some religio-philosophical veil. It is a solid and straightforward treatise on the development of not just a Kata, but entire systems of Karate-Do. It is a slow process, but a highly rewarding one.

Michael "Miko" Walker, Yondan
Tesshi, Stylistic Heir Apparent
Nahashu Ryu Karate-Do

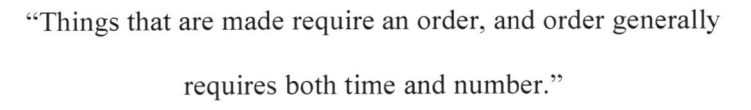

"Things that are made require an order, and order generally requires both time and number."

Ambrose (Letter to Horontianus AD 387)

Introduction

Although not heard of often, the subject of creating Kata in the Karate world arises briefly at different times over the present years. Usually the idea of one creating such a fighting system is shunned by the martial arts world. Why, you may ask? It is simply taboo to trample on the sacred feet of the past masters. It seems that every time the subject is brought up, it quickly dies down with actually non informed opinions that it cannot possibly be done in the present time for lack of instructions, or for well educated understanding of what Kata actually is. It is also thought that no one can accomplish what the "ancients" did.

I have actually heard some of the reasons stated above from other karate practitioners around the world. Along with their limited ideas, it seems that there lacks a desire to stand up and do the research on the part of these practitioners who remain satisfied to practice what Kata they already know. Many who do not even understand what Kata is for, and why it is so important to self defense. Any number of reasons is given for not creating one's own Kata, but few reasons are given by the meek to counter their suggestion.

I decided to stand up and be counted, to put my neck on the line, to offer myself up to criticism and ridicule, and do the research and write the contents within this book. The true essence of Kata has been explored by many great practitioners over the last fifty or so years. The age of modern karate wasn't even started until 1922, so some of the mind set of karate as being "ancient" is far from the truth. In this book though, the scope will be limited to that of the creation of the kata and how one can create their own just like the masters from the past. What makes creating Kata hard is the lack of knowledge on the subject that was left behind by the past masters. It is the current martial artists that, like archaeologists, have dug through time and sifted through the known Kata with careful eyes, and learned both how to take apart and put back together Kata that enable us to now bring it into written form. It does not belong to just one practitioner, but to many who have researched and discovered various ideas that have become factual through trial and error, that we can now take the final step in creating our own Kata. Like many discoveries, it is the work of many people who have taken knowledge and research from their predecessors, utilized it, and discovered something more of the puzzle. This is why I now feel comfortable enough to share what I consider to be the final step in understanding all of the questions about creating your own Kata, and to offer my humble advice on how to do it.

Before we can continue on though, we must answer the question "Why do we need to create any new Kata?" This is the question I hear most, especially from traditional practitioners of karate. You might find it interesting to know that there are several answers to this question. I will list what I believe to be the most important and significant ones to our cause, and then explain each.

1. **Knowledge is power.**
2. **Reaching the goal is superior to the goal itself.**

3. **Properly creating your own Kata (fighting system) in the ancient way continues the correct tradition of the past masters.**
4. **It motivates you to learn more Kata.**
5. **Your overall karate ability will improve.**

1. Knowledge is power.

   In order to do something right, one must know what they are doing. The more information that you have about whatever you are going to do, the better you are going to do it. Your success in completing any task in life depends on how much you know about it. If you wanted to be a Heart Surgeon, obviously you would follow the courses of study from elementary and high school through college and med school. Then you would serve as an intern and then study in your specialized medical field. In this case, heart surgery. This would still not be enough though. If you wanted to be the best Heart Surgeon in the world, you would devote all of the time that you had to that field of study. You would use all of the knowledge that you gained in twenty years of school, plus all the surgical procedures you've done, accompanied with all the medical conferences, patient care, and peer work that you could get involved with. You would always seek out new and better ways to help your patients with heart disease. Then, one day, you might even come up with a new break through procedure that could save millions of lives. This major accomplishment could not have been made possible without the power of all the knowledge that you accumulated through the years. You would be standing on the foundation of your knowledge base and on the shoulders of all those medical personnel who came before you.

To be the best, you have to put in the time and sweat to be sure, but you must have the knowledge in order to complete the task. Knowledge gives you the power to be better in any area of study. In creating your own Kata, you will gain more insight and definitely more knowledge in the art of karate. Anything that helps you study and learn something about the art of karate will enhance and improve your martial arts skills. So knowledge is the first reason why we want to learn to create a Kata like the masters from the past.

2. Reaching for the goal is superior to the goal itself.

Sound confusing? It really isn't. I think back to when the goal was to earn my black belt. It seemed like such a long and intimidating journey when I was wearing my white belt. I went through each requirement for each rank slowly. I had lots of trouble with Kata. I learned my required ones slowly. I worked with many different people along the way to black belt. People who were higher in rank then me would spend time helping me with technique and new material. My peers and I would get together to work things out. I learned lots from different black belts. I even watched as some of my peers and seniors dropped out of the class. I too, felt at times that I wanted to quit. I kept going though. Through all the pain, I gained. I made some great friends and learned a lot about karate. I passed my tests and even was passed over for advancement a couple of times. There were times when my sensei would look at me and say "You're not ready yet." Every time though, he would always encourage me to work harder and to keep going.

The day I received my black belt is still one of the best days ever in my life. It was the culmination of all the material I had learned to that point in my karate career. My mind felt like it had all this great knowledge swimming around inside of it. Of course, it did. I realize now that I had all the basics necessary to become a very good martial artist. I also realized that achieving the goal of black belt was not the important thing. It was the journey on the way to reaching the rank of black belt that was important. Yes, the belt is the sign of knowledge and ability, but, it also signifies the journey you took to get it. You may also not realize it, but it also signifies the journey you're on and the journey that is yet to come. It is the journey that is important and not the goal reached, because it is in the journey that we live our karate. It is a never ending circle of knowledge. The journey always goes on and never ends. Within it you live your life and that is why the journey is superior to reaching the goal itself.

3. Properly creating your own Kata (fighting system) in the ancient way continues the correct tradition of the past masters.

Many people have said that creating new Kata today is unnecessary. Or, that it's a waste of time since all the techniques that we need to defend ourselves are already found in the many existing Kata from the past. I disagree with this way of thinking.

Although we may not come up with any new techniques in defending ourselves, we can come up with different ways in which we use the already existing techniques. Additionally, we make them our own by manipulating them to work for our defensive purposes. Research by other martial art practitioner's shows that Kata is and was an individual's fighting system and not a groups. When we learn Kata from the past such as Naihanchi (Tekki), or Seisan, we are learning someone's fighting system. What we do by creating our own Kata is develop our own fighting system using the traditional ways that the past masters did. That is why it is said that we "continue the correct tradition". Explorers, historians, and Archaeologists love to discover the past. It is even better when they unlock the secrets of how something was done. It makes them feel as if they are there at that time period in history doing the same thing as the ancients. This is the romanticism of the research and it causes a very satisfied feeling. Likewise, by discovering how to create Kata in the traditional manner can give us a sort of satisfaction that cannot be explained.

By learning existing Kata we only understand half of the process. We must learn to develop our own Kata to get all of the knowledge and complete the circle of the way of Kata. Discovering bunkai (applications) in existing Kata by reverse engineering is great, but by developing our own and putting them together properly in a fixed Kata is the whole essence of karate. Karate is Kata and Kata is karate.

4. It motivates you to learn more Kata.

Creating Kata in the tradition of the past masters gives you a new perspective on the already existing Kata. You will feel a strong desire to learn more existing Kata because of the knowledge you gained in creating your own. You will be able to "pull" more techniques out of existing Kata and use them more effectively and efficiently for a variety of self defense scenarios. Your understanding of how techniques work will quicken your knowledge.

It is not necessary to know any, or for that matter, many Kata, in order to create your own. It is necessary to know techniques, body movement, and vital areas of the human body. Also, the rules for creating the Kata are never to be omitted if you wish to do it as it was done in the past. Obviously, it is better to know karate basics and some Kata because you will relate it all much better when working with your own Kata. I recommend that one with the rank of Shodan (first degree black belt), should understand better the work involved in this project.

Once again, your drive to learn will increase because of the work that you will put into creating your own Kata. Thus, you will want to learn others in order to discover their fighting techniques. Remember though, each Kata can be studied for years before it is "milked" of its many techniques. There are enough existing Kata from the past to keep one busy for several life times.

5. Your overall karate ability will improve.

By creating your own Kata you will be constantly analyzing every aspect of its construction. You will be working with old techniques and discovering new ones on your own. You will pay close attention to the function of stances combined with your techniques and the specifics of your body's movement. Making adjustments and learning what movements should be hard, and which should be soft (internal/external), along with creating the form of structure in order to perform your new Kata, all will benefit your over all karate ability.

Any time you can slow it all down and think it through, you will have a deeper understanding of whatever it is that you do. Like the piano player practicing a hard passage in a concerto, we must slow it all down to "see" and understand it all. Our body must know the correct positioning and delivery of the technique. Our mind must understand the technique and its ability to the fullest. Only then can we begin to gradually build up the speed and power required to perform it correctly. We learn to move slow, against our desire to move fast, so that we may become better and more efficient at our karate. By creating our own Kata we are forced to slow down. It takes a long time to produce your own fighting system. Thus our over all karate ability improves.

Hopefully these five reasons stated above for why we would or should create new Kata will be enough to spark your interest to continue on to read this book and experiment with it yourself. Remember, Kata is the finished product. It's the "end" that we have without knowing how it got to "be". Once again, it's like the archaeologist discovering a new artifact and not knowing what it was used for. He must look deeper into the object and one of the ways he does that is by creating his own. In this way he discovers more answers about what the object is, what it was used for, and its capabilities. In doing this he is forced to answer more questions that also arise. Thus, more knowledge is acquired while newer questions push us to further study and limits. We must do this with the Kata we have by first taking it apart by reverse engineering, or more traditionally speaking, by using the rules of Kasai. This will give us information on how it was put together, and even more on why no movement was wasted, but instead vital to the whole. Then we can begin to build or create our own Kata or if you prefer, fighting system. Then we will have the whole of Kata and not just the half. We must graduate from our Bachelors, to our Masters, and finally become Professors in our fighting system of karate and its Kata.

Kata Transmission

There are many different ways of saying the same thing. Anyone who has experience as any kind of a teacher can attest to this fact. Whether a school teacher or a parent, each knows that the range of imparting knowledge to each other takes on many forms. All forms of instruction produce the individual known as a teacher.

Teachers learn early on in their careers that students learn in different ways. All people are different. How someone understands or grasps a concept can be very different then someone else. In fact, a room full of students listening to the same teacher, explaining a certain principle, may produce only a third of the class in understanding the material the first time it is introduced. The teacher always has to repeat the process not only the same way, but in a variety of ways. Once again, people learn in different ways.

Some students are auditory learners. They pick up or understand the material they are being taught simply by listening to the spoken word or directions. Others only do well by demonstration. These are the visual learners. Still, some must have more of hands on experience. They have to participate in the process. They must "do" the lesson physically in order to learn. There are those students who must take a certain amount of time to think and process the information that was given to them in order to understand it. There are many ways in which all of us may learn something.

Although we may use most all of our senses in learning material taught to us, it is a proven fact that one "sense" will over-ride the others in each of the before mentioned ways above. Not to be left out of course, are those who form the exception to that statement. Those are the individuals that learn only by a combination of all the methods that people learn by. Not one sense is stronger then the other in these students. There is no dominant trait.

Add in the medical or psychological problems that exist (blindness, deafness, ADD, ADHD, etc.) and teachers are left with additional concerns on how to impart their lessons. All of these "ways" of learning give us an idea as to how communication is the vital link in imparting ideas and knowledge from one human being to another. Although none of these learning areas have been discussed in any great detail; and some such as culture and language have been left off of the list, the reader should now have a fairly good understanding as to why there are many ways of saying the same thing.

This is very true when looking at the definitions of the title of this chapter, "Kata Transmission". I have seen varied ways in which the word Kata has been defined in my 30 years as a martial artist. Each individual who has tried to convey its meaning has put into words the way in which they want to transmit their understanding of it. I am not any different then those teachers before me. I like to keep things as simple as possible. In my own understanding of the many definitions that I have read, certain facts are evident in all of them. **Therefore, my definition of the word Kata in its simplest form for me is: "An individual's fighting system comprised of all their fighting techniques, grouped together with designed movement, in order to retain and transmit that fighting system".** Some may be jumping out of their shoes right now after reading my definition and screaming that it's too simple, doesn't have enough information, or even that it's too confusing. This is fine with me as we have already discussed in this chapter how all of us understand things and learn things in their own way. My definition is what works for me and it is what forms the foundation of what this book is all about.

Here is where the purpose of this book becomes relevant. In discussing the creation of Kata in this book we will look at many different ideas, reasons, facts, and opinions about this subject from the martial arts world. One of the latest and widely accepted terms in understanding Kata is a process known as reverse engineering.

In my understanding of reverse engineering (note that I said "my understanding") it is a process of working backwards in the kata. It involves taking it apart piece by piece in order to learn how and why it was put together and used in the first place. I will discuss reverse engineering in much greater detail and at length in a later chapter of this book. Since reverse engineering is a process of working backwards and the purpose of this book is to create Kata, it is necessary that the reader gets the mindset early on that we are taking apart Kata in order to learn how to build it. The creators of Kata, individual fighting systems, left absolutely no records on how they created them. There are many, many books written by much more knowledgeable martial artists then myself on the market today that discuss this fact in great detail. So we modernists are left to dissect, if you will, the Kata they left us, and to discover their benefits or draw backs. In doing so as physicians learned the human body and its various organs functions through dissection, exploration, and study and research, we can unlock mysteries, secrets, and the ability to create our own Kata. There still will be many varied understandings of Kata though, because of the lack of written records on their creation from the past. We are left to explore. We will not all agree but hopefully we may all learn something new in our exploration. Perhaps this creating Kata journey will combine with other martial artists' ideas on how it was done. We can only guess as we may really never know. In the exploration we live the essence of Kata and Karate.

Our first step in learning to create Kata then, is to closely examine what it actually is. We must observe it, learn it, perform it, and use the basic questions of science to gain knowledge about it. These questions are who, what, why, when, where, and how that we all have learned to ask in elementary school.

Using my definition of Kata given earlier we can begin to understand the "what" that makes these forms. Any karateka (practitioner of karate) knows full well that Kata exists. Many schools require performance of different Kata by their students in order to advance in rank. It is important to note here that I am only speaking about karate and not any other forms of martial arts. Additionally, some karate schools do no focus on Kata at all. Students, when they first join a karate school, know little to nothing about karate. Some have a very basic understanding of it and have various reasons for wanting to learn it. They have no idea of the history of it and most of their knowledge about it comes from friends, television, or the movies. So a student is at the mercy of the instructor when learning about karate. Unfortunately, not even some of the instructors know their own history. This in itself is fine, but not for our purposes here. When discussing Kata it is assumed that the reader has been exposed to it in their Karate training.

The "what it is", of Kata, has been discussed for at least the last fifty years, ever since our service men brought it back from Okinawa after World War II, Karate, and in particular Kata, has been defined in many ways. I myself have heard it defined, and even been taught in the early part of my Karate career, that Kata is a dance of death, a way to fight multiple opponents at one time, just practicing basics, and a way to hide the inner secrets of the most deadly techniques of Karate. In reality I believe that there is only a little truth to each of those definitions. Kata, as we will discuss, is something much less of a mystery then it is romanticized to be. What we have progressed in from fifty years ago to today is more knowledge about Kata. As second generation and even third generation Westerners in the art of Karate, we have revisited Okinawa and learned more about it and have become better at it. It is only natural, due to the length of tours of duty, that our first Western Karate forefathers were only able to learn so much of the art itself and its essence of Kata. Since the late 1940's we have come a long way. This is not to say that we have finally made it though with a complete knowledge of Kata.

Remember, we are dealing with a verbal transmission of knowledge from instructor to student down through the centuries of fighting styles. This is the only way that Kata was passed on to individuals. The fighting systems of a family, or an individual were closely guarded secrets and were only shared with other family members or with very devout and close friends. This is where the secrecy may have come in and gained its over romanticized theory today. It was simply a way for the founders to remember and guard their techniques that worked for them. Therefore, no written account or directions have come down to us on Kata. What they have passed on to us is a finished product with no idea of how and why it was constructed. Take into account how knowledge is transmitted and learned by individuals and you can see how it is possible to have lost some of the original information from the beginning. Once again we are dealing with how people learn things and how they teach them. Without any original written records we are dependent on the human factor.

Although the human factor has its flaws, there is some comfort in knowing that the Kata from the past has survived with probably only some slight variations. This is due to the meticulous work and understanding of the masters from the 19th century. I give them the credit simply because we do have some written records of their lives and the way that they learned, practiced, and taught their Kata. Their students were the first to write about them and their experiences. I refer here of Chojun Miyagi, Shoshin Nagamine, Choki Motobu, Kenwa Mabuni, and Gichen Funakoshi. These masters were able to tell about their instructors, their instructors' instructors, and their own experiences. Thus they were able to shed light on three generations of Karate and Kata. They brought Karate into the modern world and made it assessable to all of us. They revealed some of the so called secrets of Kata to their students, but for the most part stayed silent. They used methods of strict instruction and precise copying and repetition of their students in the performance of the Kata. They did not allow questions. Whether intentional or not, this helped to pass Kata down to us with little change. It did not allow us to unlock its mysteries however.

So we have Kata. What Kata is, lies in the varied definitions of it. All of which have common elements. Kata is a finished product of grouped fighting techniques that must be drawn out of the whole in order to answer the other questions about it. This answers the "what" Kata is.

We now find ourselves moving on to one of the other questions about Kata. In answering each of these questions, who, what, when, where, why, and how; we will see an overlapping or blending of our answers to each of them. This chapter is discussing Kata as we know it. We will slowly move into the modern day thinking about Kata and then on to the questions about creating it, and finally how to create it. We will now look at the question of where Kata was created.

Every culture in civilization has had its own fighting methods. From the time man first used his bare hands and feet (not to mention his teeth) to hurt another man, all the way down to modern technology, humans have developed warfare and fighting to a very skilled degree. Greece had its Spartans, Rome had its Garrisons, Atilla had his Huns, Britain its Royal Navy, and America its Special Forces. All were and are highly trained in the killing of other human beings. The Eastern countries were no different. Their development in culture led to a different means of fighting. The Chinese emperors had their armies that were efficient with swords, spears, and hand to hand combat. The Japanese had their warrior class known as Samurai, who had specialists in the different weapons and the hand to hand art of Ju Jutsu. Some would argue that the East progressed slowly into the modern world because it remained "locked" away from the Western explorers for so long. Some would also argue that the Eastern culture and philosophy is far superior to that of the West. Being as it may, it is within the civilian domain, and not the military, where we find what is known as Kata, developing. We know that it is in the countries of China, Okinawa, (before it became a part of Japan), and Japan where Kata was developed, most certainly first in China. Since this book is about creating Kata and not the complete history of it, the reader is encouraged to read the many books out there that give in depth historical information on the subject. The information given here is for general understanding in order to develop the building blocks, or foundation, for creating Kata. See the list of recommended books and DVD's in the appendix for detailed information on the history of Kata and the creation of Karate.

For now we must understand that it was the civilian populations of these countries that developed Kata. From the monks and peasants of China and the Shaolin temple, to the aristocrats of Okinawa, fighting arts were traded and combined to form the unique style of "Te", or hand, and eventually Karate, empty hand. It was the civilian population who needed a fighting system for it was they who had no protection from the many criminals on their streets. Combining the Chinese forms of Kung Fu with their own indigenous fighting arts, civilians could learn to defend themselves against such enemies in a country that was weak in law enforcement and during its history banned on several occasions from the use of weapons. Thus Karate Jutsu (empty hand deadly force) was developed for civilian self defense. Karate- Do only developed early in the 20th century as a means of promotion and physical education in the Okinawan school system. Kata was passed from instructor to student on Okinawa and later to Japan. It was most normally done in secret in order to protect the founders' fighting system. It was used to devastate and incapacitate an attacker and only later, when the need for such action decreased due to better social and police protection, was passed on as an art form or "way" to better one's mind, body, and spirit. The "where" that Kata was created was a combination of the Chinese forms combined with the fighting hand systems of Okinawa. Thus Okinawa is the birthplace of the Karate Kata we know today.

In answering the question "where" we now will take on the question of "who". We are overlapping our answers a bit as some mention was given to this question in the last segment. No one knows who was the very first so called inventor of Karate or more specifically, its Kata. I believe that it was developed by many different people over a long period of time. China definitely had a very heavy influence on Kata and the formation of Karate. Because of the cultural relations between Okinawa and China, the flow of information on all aspects of art and business was not hindered into the Ryu Kyu Kingdom. Thus, the people of Okinawa learned from the Chinese people their Kung Fu forms and methods of unarmed combat. When combining it with their indigenous systems, it couldn't help but develop into a system of its own. When combined with their local Tuite (grappling/joint locking) systems, the Okinawans were eventually able to develop what we know as Karate today.

For our purposes in this book, we will be looking at the Kata developed or taught by the Masters; notably, Kanryo Higgashionna, Itosu Anko, and their various students. Once again, there are many books on the market that deal with this subject. A list will be provided in the appendix of this book.

The question of when Karate was created dates back to when China and the Ryu Ku Kingdom shared their trade relations and cultural relations. This goes back to the 1600's and maybe earlier. There is no exact date as to when the very first Okinawan created his own fighting system. Karate was developed over many years in Okinawa. Modern Karate as we know it, was formed and introduced as several different styles, by some of the best practitioners of it, from the various villages or towns in Okinawa, at the end of the 19th century and the beginning of the 20th.

Why Karate was created has already been discussed earlier in this chapter, and is one of those overlapping questions that I have spoken about. It is in the "how" Karate or more specifically, Kata was created that we will now start to discuss in the following chapters. We have seen that the transmission of Kata was done from teacher to student over many years without much explanation. Due to much research from many modern Karate practitioners such as Patrick McCarthy, Iain Abernethy, Lawrence Kane, and Bill Burgar, we have learned to get at the applications of the Kata, discover its historical background and its techniques of self defense from the human acts of violence, follow transmitted rules to better understand it, and to reverse engineer it. With the abundant information that these great Karate practitioners and writers have offered us, we can now not only understand the Karate Kata, but we can learn how to create our own in the traditional manner with which the masters from the past used themselves. By combining my research with theirs, I humbly offer my transmission and construction of Karate's ultimate weapon, its Kata.

Physical Acts of Violence

When we say "physical", we are speaking of using our hands, feet, knees, legs, arms, head, fingers, teeth, and elbows. No other mechanical weapons such as a knife, club, or gun will be discussed.

Physical acts of aggression or violence are any body part used to attack another individual with the intent to do bodily harm. Some of the acts include grabbing, punching, slapping, hitting, kicking, tackling, tripping, biting, scratching, ripping, and head butting. Patrick McCarthy has discovered over 70 ways in which people use to attack another human being, and in fact, has come up with even sub-categories of those 70. All, used alone or in combinations, can do damage to any one.

At this point it should be pointed out that people who are trying to do you bodily harm are usually very experienced at what they do, and almost never attack unless the odds of winning are very high in their favor. So where does this leave us in the area of self defense?

First, by recognizing potential trouble before it happens by scanning areas, is a good self defense tactic. Another one is avoiding places that are either known as trouble spots or potential problem areas. These two self defense tactics alone can keep you out of lots of trouble without ever having to get physical. Along with these ideas I suggest carrying a cell phone to call the police. We live in a relatively safe environment with laws of order, and plenty of people assigned to enforce them. There are always the exceptions to the general norm though.

Robberies, rapes, harassment, stalking, domestic violence, and school bullies, all, unfortunately, exist. Add child abductions, sexual predators, car theft, and murder, every town USA and world wide, has their share of these problems. Break it down to arguments, sporting events, and bars, and you can see what I'm speaking about. Usually, drugs and/or alcohol play a major role in most crimes. So where does all of this put you, the nice law abiding citizen that lives a peaceful life?

It should put you in what I call "safe guard" when you are in public alone, with family, or with friends. There are times when you might be waiting in a long line to buy a drink and some obnoxious drunk individual is trying to cut in front of you. You might be at a sporting event rooting for your team and a guy who likes the other team decides he wants you out of your seat and somewhere else. You might be the coach of some ball team and an aggressive parent has lost his cool and wants to point his finger in your face and push you around to make his point and to start a fight. Or you might be the unfortunate recipient, through no fault of your own, of one of the nasty crimes listed above. Being on "safe guard", involves using the tactics of avoiding, scanning, and carrying a cell phone. As discussed though, these tactics are not always effective. Sometimes, good people get physically attacked. The way they get attacked is with some form of the physical acts of violence and almost never when you expect it.

A knee kick to the groin, a round house punch to the head, a body tackle, or a bear hug describe a few of the ways you might get attacked. Kata, was designed to deal with these physical acts of violence. In the following chapters we will see how. Knowing now what a physical act of violence is, you should be able to come up with many that an assailant can use against you. By doing this you are creating realistic attack scenarios with which you can develop effective techniques to defend against. This is how techniques were developed in the beginning of Karate. Only later, after they were used in a two man practice scenario, were they strung together to form a Kata (See McCarthy-www.koryu – uchinadi.com).

At this point we will begin a short, but very important study of the body's vital areas. You must know these as your attacker will try to hit you in them, and you must effectively counter to his in order to end a confrontation immediately, or to give you enough space in order to get away without further damage to you. As a martial artist, you should know as much about fighting as possible. Knowing the body's weak areas is vital to your fighting skill.

Following is a list from Iain Abernethy's book "Bunkai Jutsu". It is divided up by body sections and uses some of the more important vital areas which are easy to find and attack creating much pain for your assailant. First I will list some of what Kata has to offer in the way of self defense and then I will move on to the vital areas.

KATA USES

1. Strikes
2. Joint locks
3. submission holds
4. Target nerve points
5. Soft tissue destruction
6. Organ destruction
7. Throws
8. Take downs
9. Aggressive ground fighting
10. Closing distance
11. Unbalancing opponent
12. strength
13. Endurance
14. Timing
15. Spacing
16. Body shifting
17. Balance
18. Speed
19. Breathing
20. Mental alertness

These are some of the major things that Kata gives us. More can be found and listed but I believe the above will serve our purposes nicely.

Body Weaknesses/Vital Areas

HEAD

1. Coronal Structure – top of head – Tendo
2. Frontal Fontunel – Top of forehead
3. Temple – Kasumi
4. Orbital Bones – Surrounds eye – Seidon
5. Eyes – Gansei
6. Glabella – Between eyebrows – Uto
7. Philtrum – Below nose, above gum line – Jinchu
8. Center of Jaw – right below lower lip – Gekon
9. Lower edge of jaw – Mikazuki
10. Cavity behind the ear – Dokko
11. Third intervertebral space – under base of skull on center of neck – Keicha
12. Carotid Sinus – side of neck – Matsukaze
13. Superstructural notch – front of neck below throat and above sternum – Hichu

TORSO

1. Collar bones – Murasami
2. Xiphoid Process – lower end of sternum – Kyosen

3. Solar Plexus – just below sternum – suigetsu
4. Fifth and Sixth Thoracic vertebrae – center of back level with lower end of shoulder blades – Kassatsu
5. Subaxillary region – side of rib cage under armpit between muscles of chest and back – Kyoei
6. Fifth and Sixth Ribs – both sides of body directly below nipples, end of ribs – Ganka
7. Seventh Intercostal Space – both sides of body, four inches across from solar plexus – Denko
8. Lower back – kidneys, both sides of lower back – Ushiro Denko
9. Floating Ribs – lower part of rib cage either side of the body – Inazuma
10. Lower Abdomen – One inch below naval – Tanden
11. Coccyx – tip of spine or tail bone – Bitei
12. Testicles – Kinteki

ARMS AND HANDS

1. Upper arm – outside of arm below shoulder muscle between biceps and triceps – Wanjun
2. Elbow – one inch up from tip of elbow, funny bone – Chukitsu
3. Inside of Wrist inside of elbow between radius and ulna, one inch up from crease of wrist – Uchi Shakutaku
4. Outside of Wrist – just up from back of wrist – Soto Shakutaku

5. Back of Hand – between thumb and index finger between knuckles and ring and pinky – Shuko

LEGS AND FEET
1. Inguinal Region – front of leg where thigh joins torso – Yako
2. Sciatic Nerve – a back of leg below the buttocks – Ushiro Inazuma
3. Vasuts Lateralis – half way down outside of thigh – Fukuto
4. Lower Calf – lower part of calf – Kusanagi
5. Instep – top of foot – Kori

Studying these important vital points of the body will help you to better defend yourself if you are ever in scuffle or a fight for your life. The creators of Kata knew the human body well and all of its strong and weak areas.

Techniques

Techniques are the original responses or receivers, that you put together in order to stop a physical act of violence from being performed on you. There can be many, or just a few, that deal with a particular act of violence. You, the creator, are in charge of that. You are limitless in your creation of techniques. How well they work is also your responsibility. I believe a technique is only good if it leaves your attacker in a position where they are totally at a severe disadvantage. This disadvantage could mean anything from escaping from them and fleeing, to totally devastating the attacker physically.

I like to use a common threefold tried-and-true formula for my techniques. This formula is, close the distance, unbalance the opponent, and devastate the opponent. Think of this as receiving the attacker. Not all of you reading this will agree with the formula I just listed and you are correct, it will not work in every situation. It does work in most of them though. There is no, one kind of technique that can deal with all attack situations, but keeping in mind the three principles listed above will help you in most. We'll briefly discuss each of these three principles now.

1. Closing the Distance.

    Being close to your attacker makes you stronger. Your arms are not overextended and are closer to your body's center of gravity. Try this with a partner: Facing each other stand one arms length away from him. Now have your partner grab your left wrist with his right hand. Now you try a simple wrist escape by pulling your left hand away from his grasp. Make sure you use only your left hand. Notice the difficulty in doing this. Now repeat the same exercise but this time stand closer to one another. Did you notice how much easier it was to release from his grab? This is because your captured arm was closer to your center. This gave you the use of your whole body in escaping and not just your left arm. Of course, you never want to let anyone get a good hold on you. If at all possible, you want to stay out of an attacker's range. Unfortunately, bad guys don't tell you when they're going to attack. It's almost always a surprise. Even when you notice it, the attack may come too quickly for you to be out of range and flee. So if you get attacked you must increase your strength by closing the distance. Of course, this can benefit your attacker as well, but our second principle will handle that.

2. Unbalance the Attacker.

At close range to your opponent we have demonstrated that you are stronger in a limb capture situation simply because your limbs are closer to your core, the center of your gravity. While this is true, you must also realize that your attacker will be stronger also, unless you do something to gain the advantage over him. It is not good enough to be equal with your attacker. You must be better then the attacker in all aspects of fighting once the initial threat has started. If you do not take control of the entire situation, you will without doubt lose, and it might be your life that you lose! Therefore, you must go from being a passive ordinary person to the full out aggressor in your defense. So the second principle that I use is to unbalance your attacker. Keep in mind that with the three principles that I am discussing, it is important that they must be used in conjunction with each other. They are not stand alone techniques but are principles that make great techniques. These principles make the individual techniques from your Kata work. Without using them in combination, the technique you have chosen to use will simply not work. Each of the three principles is a part of the technique you have chosen and are based on scientific principles.

Once you have closed the distance with your technique, you must immediately unbalance your opponent in order to put him in a weak position. He must feel out of control so that he's thinking about regaining it instead of continuing his attack. This gives you the advantage to now be the aggressor or the one in charge, and to complete your technique while he is caught up in being unbalanced. You now have the superior position and can finish him off by completing your technique.

To demonstrate this "unbalance", I will use the first move from the Kata Seiyunchin. Like the previous example, have your training partner stand in front of you and grab your left wrist with his right hand (same side grab). Making the technique work for the situation, cross your right hand over your left and grab your partners hand on the pinky side. Once you've grabbed his hand, step your right foot back 45 degrees from the front into Shiko Dachi (Sumo Stance), while simultaneously returning your right hand to the chambered position with his right hand in it.

When you study this technique we can see that by grabbing our partner's right hand with our right hand and returning it to chamber, we have twisted his arm into a painful position while also twisting his wrist. At the same time while stepping back into a 45 degree Shiko Dachi with the right leg, we have performed two of the three techniques needed to make any technique work. We have successfully closed the distance to our opponent and have brought him off balance. The step back with his arm twisted has caused our training partner to bend forward at the waist rendering him off balance because we have lowered our center of gravity and his captured arm is part of our body now. Thus he is now in a very unstable position and our technique can finish with the third principle.

3. Devastate Your Attacker.

Any technique drawn from any known Kata should end with the destruction of your attacker. At the very least, it should leave your attacker in such a state that they will not be able to continue their assault on you; and they will not want to anyway. With this in mind remember that techniques were developed first before they were arranged into Kata. These techniques were meant to stand alone and be all that is needed to defeat any opponent given the Act of Violence that was being used against you. In other words, techniques that work against a kick to your mid-section will not work against a grabbing maneuver by an attacker. The right technique must be used in the right situation. Keep in mind, once again, that a given technique has everything in it needed to finish or end an attack. They each were carefully put together so that people who knew them could defend themselves from unwanted and unwarranted aggression.

Let's continue on with our last example. At this point you have closed the distance to your training partner and have taken his center away and unbalanced him. He is leaning over and close to you because of the stance you moved into and the arm control of his right arm that you have on him. If we follow the technique from the Kata Seiyunchin in this example, we will next use a type of finger thrust on our partner. In the position that our training partner is in, there are lots of vulnerable vital points on his body left open for us to take advantage of. To name a few, his whole right side rib cage is exposed, under his right arm is exposed, the whole right side of his head, face, and neck is exposed, and even the right side of his back is exposed. Any one of these areas has sufficient vital areas on them to do enough damage on any attacker to stop the attack and allow you to flee the scene and the danger. In our example we are using a finger thrust, but we can use any strike with our left hand that we wish because of the position our partner is in and the type of area we want to attack. So, by using this one technique from the Kata Seiyunchin, we can see the many possibilities to end the confrontation. Additionally, if you study this one technique you will discover that it is effective against other acts of violence as well.

So there we have it. Mostly all the techniques found in the Kata demonstrate these three principles. If you keep this in mind, you will not only be able to discover other effective techniques from the Kata you already know, but you will be able to use and develop your own for use in creating your own Kata. Realistically, there probably isn't a technique that you can come up with that is new. However, you can choose and combine what works best for your fighting system and placement in your Kata.

You must know and develop many techniques. Use the ones that you want, but I suggest you try to utilize some that have applications for varied situations. Such as, joint locks and strikes. These can be advanced techniques within your own Kata.

By working through the creative process, one always benefits by learning more. Both through your mistakes and failures as well as successes, you live the experience of true Karate. The final product then becomes all yours.

Understand the meaning of the techniques you already know, and learn and create more for your own use. This is the key ingredient for creating your own Kata.

Reverse Engineering

It is assumed that the karate practitioner reading this book has some experience in Karate and can perform one or two Kata. If you have no experience, you will understand the following in theory, but will not be able to grasp and apply it in any practice.

As stated by Bill Burgar in his book Five Years One Kata, on page 105, "Reverse Engineering is a term used to describe the act of figuring out what a product does by just looking at or taking the object apart. There are no instructions, or design specifications to read in order to understand how the product works, or was constructed. Reverse Engineering requires different skills than the original engineering process and it is always easy to make the wrong assumptions about what something is for and go down a blind alley".

As I stated in chapter one, the transmission of Kata was done from teacher to student. Nothing in history has been discovered that shows that Kata was passed down any other way then orally. No written records were kept, and there was no modern technology around to record it. So all we have is a finished product in the Kata itself. Our job is to de-construct it in hopes of finding its techniques and what each was probably designed for. Finding the techniques and their movement from the Kata is known as the Katas' Bunkai.

There is no way to know if we have the correct usage of the intended technique from any Kata. We can probably come close to the creators' idea, but it is really just an educated guess. Given the many common acts of human physical violence, it is definitely assured that one technique can handle a variety of attacks. While testing the chosen technique we will inevitably stumble onto the creators' original use for it. We just won't know it for logical reasons stated earlier.

The seriousness of looking at the technique selected from your chosen kata cannot be expressed enough. One must pay close attention to the placement of the hands and feet as well as the head and the angles of movement. You must keep in mind that the technique you have chosen is in its finished state, that is, what you see is the ending of the technique. You must take this technique backwards at least one kata movement in order to get to the beginning of it. This is where you must look to see how each part of the body moves in order to get into its ending position. Only then can you start to figure out the chosen techniques' purposes. With this in mind, pay close attention to where the feet are starting from and into which stance they finish. Watch to see if there is an angled, straight or backward movement. Maybe the feet move sideways. Is there a height difference from where the technique started and where it ended? Are the arms in a different position, and if they are, do they seem to be attacking, grasping, blocking, pushing, or pulling? Does the head of your body end up differently? Pay attention to the slightest details in your chosen technique. It is from these that you will find many defenses that the technique can be utilized for.

Now that you have some knowledge of how to reverse engineer a kata, and have taken a look at some of its techniques the correct way, you must experiment with each of them to see if, how, and why, they might flow from one to another. By doing this you might discover that one technique leads to another at certain points in a kata in order to handle an attack scenario that you haven't thought of yet. I'm certain that you will discover many, many uses for the techniques from the kata you have chosen. For single attack defense and offense, to ground fighting, submission holds, and vital area attacks; using techniques together or alone, or even parts of a technique will give you many defensive ideas and teach you why one kata equals one persons complete fighting system.

While working backwards (reverse engineering), through your chosen kata, pay close attention to movements within the kata. For instance, how many steps forward or backwards are there, repetitive techniques, slow, medium, and fast movement? Even seemingly useless moves all will help you in learning how to construct your own kata.

Reverse engineering is essential for the purpose of creating your own kata. Without this process you will never be able to correctly understand techniques or learn their proper usage.

Hidden Rules

Sometimes you will find that one technique does not answer all of the necessary questions to make it a workable technique. These questions are the rules given earlier in this book: Closing the distance, unbalance the opponent, and totally devastating them. If you find a technique in a kata that only answers the first, or the first two of the rules, but does not utilize them all, then look to the next technique in the kata that follows the one you're working on. Most always this second technique will complete the rules and make the whole extremely effective. If it does not work, then it's back to the drawing board on your chosen technique. You might then decide to go to the technique before your chosen technique and approach it all differently. Patience is the key and with it you will be rewarded with lots of workable techniques.

By working with Reverse Engineering you will also begin to understand how kata were created. This then, is essential for our goal in this book. Altogether, reverse engineering utilizes the rules of "Kasai" as revealed by Goju Ryu teacher Seikeichi Toguchi and expounded upon in Lawrence Kane and Chris Wilders' book "The Way of Kata". These very important rules follow here and are taken from their book pages 139 – 141.

The Rules of Kasai

1. Do not be deceived by the enbusen line.
2. Advancing techniques imply attack, while retreating techniques imply defense.
3. There is only one enemy at a time and he is in front of you.
4. Every movement in kata has martial meaning and can be used in a real fight.
5. A hand returning to chamber usually has something in it.
6. Utilize the shortest distance to your opponent.
7. Control your opponents' head and you control the opponent.
8. There is no block.
9. Kata demonstrate the proper angles.
10. Touching your own body in kata indicates touching your opponent.
11. Contour the body- strike hard to soft and soft to hard.
12. There is no pause.

As stated in his book "Goju Ryu II", Seikichi Toguchi received these rules from Goju Ryu founder and karate master, Chojun Miyagi before his death in 1953. Toguchi was told that the first three rules were the "main" or "basic" rules of "kasai" (the work with which one deciphers any kata application), and the last nine are the supplementary or advanced rules. Thus the rules were twofold in process. The first three rules known to the masters as "shuyo san gensoko" (main or basic), and the last nine rules as "hosoko joko" (supplementary or advanced). The entire process was known as kasai no genri (the theory of kasai). Toguchi received these rules and was asked to keep them secret by Miyagi. As explained by Kane and Wilder in "The Way of Kata", the past masters kept these rules as a closely guarded secret and shortly before they passed on would reveal them to a senior student. Seeing no need to keep them secret any longer, Toguchi revealed the first three in his "Goju Ryu II" book published in 2001. These first three of the twelve kasai he made widely known and kept the last nine only for his close circle of friends or students.

It is my opinion that the combination of the publication of the first three rules of Kasai and the studies on reverse engineering by authors and practitioners such as Patrick McCarthy, Bill Burgar, and Iain Abernethy, (to name only a few), helped to make Toguchi sensei realize that it was time to let the only real "secret" of the kata out. Thus Kane and wilder have published them in their traditional manner (so to speak), in their book "The Way of Kata" as students of the late teacher.

I will give a brief descriptive summary of each of these rules and discuss the two part separation of the first three and the last nine here. I will then explain how to create your own kata from these rules organized in a different manner in the next chapters of this book.

The first three rules known as *shuyo san gensoku* are the main principles of the Kasai No Genri and form the foundation for our looking at how kata can be created. These rules were not made up by any karate practitioner of the modern era, but rather were passed down sparingly from Master to student. The following are from Teguchi Sensei as given him by Miyagi Chojun Shihan, the founder of Goju Ryu Karate Do.

1. **Don't be deceived by the Enbusen Rule**.

    The Enbusen, or line of direction, that a kata follows is just that. It is a performance line designed simply to perform the strung together techniques of each kata on. This line interestingly, covers all eight compass directions. The reason for this directional line is so that a kata may be practiced in a limited amount of space. It is my opinion that unless outside, the creators did not have much space to work with indoors. Therefore, space was saved by changing directions in order to fit the kata in the limited space available to the creators and practitioners of kata. This is why masters such as Gichen Funakoshi wrote in his book "Karate Jutsu" that "elaborate facilities and equipment are not required", and that "It is flexible to modification". In my opinion, kata can be practiced any where and in any space by modifying the stances to meet the space allotted. There is however an interesting discovery that needs to be mentioned here. As mentioned earlier, many techniques can be derived from kata by reverse engineering. Some have noticed, and rightfully so, that by simply changing a direction at the end of seemingly one technique is actually the beginning of a whole different technique or a continuation to the finishing of a technique. This can be seen simply by moving from a right foot forward long stance with a right handed middle punch, to reversing to the rear by moving the right foot around and ending up facing the back in the same position with the same foot but now with a right hand lower block. Your right hand might have something in it (in this case we'll say an opponent's arm), when you begin to move towards the rear reversing your direction and thus pulling your opponent off balance or putting them in a position that will set them up for a devastating blow. This can be seen in the Pinan Nidan (Heian Shodan) kata. When a kata changes direction, everything must be considered. Additionally, kata movement has been seemingly regulated to no more than three or four steps in any one direction before returning in the same direction or changing its direction entirely.

2. **Advancing techniques imply attack, while retreating techniques imply defense.**

Regardless of what technique you are performing, the creators of kata made a point that moving forward would mean that you are attacking an opponent and that moving back would indicate a defensive technique. Even while studying any specific kata, if it appears that a block is being utilized in a forward movement, it should be considered an attack and with further study any student will soon see this. Even though there is no such thing as retreating in karate, moving backward indicates a drawing in of an opponent or the completion of a technique by putting an opponent in a certain position.

3. There is only one enemy and he/she is in front of you.

This is very important for our purposes. There is no indication that kata was ever developed to fight multiple opponents. Kata is a means to practice each of the techniques within the kata, and although there is a form of kata bunkai that was developed by modern masters placing individuals in the different directions of the kata so that the performer can do the kata demonstrating its outward techniques, this does not imply the true meaning of the kata. When you practice your kata, you should believe that you have only one opponent, and he/she is standing right in front of you.

Each technique within any kata can be taken out of the kata and a two man tandem exercise can be practiced utilizing the chosen technique. Fighting many people at the same time utilizing a certain kata is in itself totally ridiculous, as this means that each person fighting you would have to comply with what your techniques are in the kata. This only works in movies and on television and in the minds of the under educated teachers and practitioners of karate.

Although not equally split, this concludes the first half of the twelve rules of Kasai No Genri. These first three rules are once stated again, the main rules of kasai. In themselves they reveal some very big truths about some well known mis-understandings throughout the karate world. They shed a big light on kata right from the beginning of our study in creating it.

The second half of Kasai No Genri is the *Hosoku Joko* or the supplemental rules. There are nine of these and each is very important to creating kata as they are in dissecting or reverse engineering the kata to find techniques. None were created to be overlooked by the masters. In doing so, you would have pieces missing to the complete puzzle and it would only leave us guessing; something I'm sure none of us wishes to do in our pursuit of the importance of kata.

4. **Every movement in kata has martial meaning/significance and can be used in a real fight.**

I find it very interesting and notable that the word "sport" does not appear in rule number four above. The word instead is "martial" and martial means military and deadly fighting, or war like, as defined by Webster's New Collegiate Dictionary. So, if every movement in kata has a deadly fighting meaning, then it stands that kata, and the many techniques that make it up must be deadly. Thus, kata training and the discovery of techniques in the kata, must be taken with the utmost seriousness. We are dealing with things which can kill other human beings. You must have this mindset when you are looking for techniques from kata, or you are utilizing your own to create a kata. As Kline and Wilder state, "There were no competitions or sports tournaments; only life and death struggles to survive.

Without the benefit of modern medicine, even slight injuries in combat could become fatal, so fights had to be ended quickly" (pg 140).

5. **A hand returning to chamber usually has something in it.**

When you think about it, while watching a fight, do you ever see either opponent have one hand not in use unless it is severely injured? My guess is no. So it is only reasonable to investigate that a hand returning to a chambered position in a kata must be part of some technique. Remember, you must look at every little aspect of your kata and learn that no movement is wasted. Usually the chambered hand has some body part of the opponent in it, such as an arm, leg, or head. Its use can be for grabs, take downs, locks, joint dislocations, throws, or just to immobilize the opponent's use of that particular body part which was grabbed.

6. **Utilize the shortest distance to your opponent.**

I like to use a self defense exercise in my karate dojo that's called "Going Ballistic". This exercise is particularly useful for children and women. It also works for men. The main idea of the exercise is to go completely wild, like an animal being taken captive. This means that if you are attacked, or especially grabbed, you start everything in motion. You should immediately start throwing elbows, knees, short kicks, foot stomps, gouges, pinches, and biting, head-butting, and continuous circular, up and down, side to side movement in order to get away while causing as much offensive damage to your opponent as necessary. This means that you must be at a close range to your attacker. It also means that while you are doing this you will leave no doubt that some strike or attack that you use will be closest to some part of your attacker's body. This rule simply means to attack your opponent with whatever limb you have closest to their body. It is the shortest distance and thus the quickest way to cause some damage to your opponent. Although my "Going Ballistic" exercise is done in a very controlled environment, my students see how effective it can be, and if you have practiced a lot of techniques well, you will utilize them automatically with "mushin", no mind. By practicing in this way, all and any techniques are put into play and although my attacker may have grabbed my throat, my knee might be closest to his groin. So while I need to breathe quickly in order to stay conscious, I will simultaneously be utilizing my whole body in the escape process in order to get away and end the attack. So if my knee is closest to my attacker's groin, then that's what he's going to feel first while my hands and other parts of my body are in motion searching and hitting other targets as well while I am freeing his or her hands from my throat. Sometimes if not all times, we don't have enough time to think of which part of our body is the closest to our opponent. So going "all out" will almost guarantee that you hit the closest target with your closest weapon.

7. **Control an opponent's head and you control the opponent.**

Just sitting here counting in my mind, I can come up with 18 vital points located on my head, face, and neck of my body alone. This alone tells me that there are a lot of opportunities to do damage in one small and easily accessible area of the body. If I can successfully make contact with at least two of these areas, I know that I can win a confrontation. The reason is that the vital points in the head control breathing, vision, and motion. Additionally, if I can grab the head and turn it one way or the other, the entire body will follow in that direction. If it doesn't, the neck will break causing total paralysis or death.

8. **There is no block.**

The word "block" implies no action other then to stop something from going somewhere. It means to get in the way. With this in mind, if you just miss your block, then you're in danger of getting hit. If however, what you are used to calling a block has more then just the meaning of stopping or getting in the way of something, it then becomes something else. It becomes active and also aggressive. The Japanese word "uke" means to receive. In karate it has been utilized to mean block, but the real meaning is to receive something. In this case a strike or other attack coming at you. If your reception is placed well and utilizes the same power as your strikes, then your so called blocks become formidable weapons. To receive an attack means that you absorb the energy of the force and misdirect it to your benefit while emitting your own force during the reception. If you can do this effectively, it will make your opponent think twice about his next attack, or it can stop the confrontation without you ever having to go on the offensive. You already have with your "uke".

9. Kata demonstrate the proper angles.

As stated earlier, many techniques are embedded within each kata, and all moves have martial meaning and significance. Therefore, if a kata demonstrates a technique at a certain angle, it should be remembered that your opponent is right in front of you. If this is true, then you will always be "square" on to your opponent. This is not always the most effective place to be. What it actually means is that it is the angle that you are to your opponent and not where he is. In other words, you've already adjusted your angle and have completed your technique. Remember, you are working backwards in the kata to figure out the techniques. So the positions you find yourself in are the ending positions of the techniques. Again, how you are facing is your reaction to an opponent's attack. All creators took this into account when they created their fighting systems. The angle to your opponent that you end up in gives you the most advantage on your opponent.

10. Touching your own body in kata indicates touching your opponent.

The only reason that your hand should touch your own body and be immobile is if it is injured. You need all of your weapons available for use in a fight. So if a kata shows a hand touching your body it means that something of your opponent's is in that hand performing a lock, hold, or some other incapacitating maneuver.

11. Contour the body; strike hard to soft and soft to hard.

Whichever vital target that you are aiming for in a fight will determine what type of attack to use. The kata demonstrate different strikes that are aimed at specific targets. If the intended target is soft, then an elbow or hammer fist may be shown, if the intended vital point is hard, then a palm heel or ridge hand might be demonstrated.

12. There is no pause.

Once again, kata are a combination of many techniques put together in a specific way in order to pass down someone's fighting method. These rules help us to understand each kata better. Pauses in any kata usually demonstrate a change or emphasis in techniques at a given point. In real life fighting there is no pause. One therefore, is for performance and emphasis, while the other is to save your life. No pause.

This concludes our discussion on the twelve rules of Kasai. We will now look at how we can utilize these rules in a different order to help us create our own kata.

Creating the Past

Now that we have taken a look at the twelve rules of Kasai, we are ready to start the process of creating our own Kata. How we do this is by meticulously rearranging the rules and utilizing a well known Kata from the past to see if our new rules make sense in copying the known Kata. If they seem sensible, then we will have a blue print for how to create our own Kata. Before we begin this process though, a short story needs to be told.

The founder of Matsubayashi Shorin Ryu, Shoshin Nagamine, states in his book "The Essence of Okinawan Karate Do", that he and Chojun Miyagi, the founder of Goju Ryu Karate Do, were asked to construct some basic Kata for the Okinawa school system because the kata from Naha and Shuri Te were too hard for these beginners. Two of the kata created, Fukyu Gata Ichi and Fukyu Gata Ni, were sanctioned by Gen Hawakenwa, the Governor of the Okinawa prefecture in 1940 to be used in the school system.

Both of these kata remain today and are practiced in both the Shorin Ryu and Goju Ryu styles. Fukyu Gata Ni, for example, is better known as Gekisai Dai Ichi from Goju Ryu. The term Fukyu meaning "basic", shows that traditional karate needed to be scaled down in order to teach a wider more numerous, and younger type of student. Along with the Taikiyoku, Hookyu, Gekiha, kata from other Goju Ryu styles and Shotokan, we can see that the founders of each style deemed it very necessary to create basic kata for their students. Karate was now launched in the modern world and was taught to many at one time instead of in the traditional way of one on one or two. Thus, the classical kata from the cities of Shuri and Naha needed time to develop. To help this, various instructors created the basic kata to develop techniques that would later be found in the classical kata.

The fact that the mayor of the Okinawa prefecture chose two kata to be used in the school system proves that there were at least several to choose from. Thus, Nagamini and Miyagi knew how to create kata on their own. Even though their kata are deemed basic or beginner's kata today, they still have a standard set of bunkai (applications) that are taught with them. Additionally, many bunkai applications can be found in them that meet the criteria for devastating an attacker. I myself have utilized many that I have found in Fukyu Gata Ni (Geki Sai Dai Ichi), in my personal training and instruction.

The need for basic kata being evident in 1940, and the creation of basic kata by the karate styles founders, indicates their knowledge on how to create kata in the traditional manner. They acknowledged the need for their creation and went about their work utilizing their well kept secrets on how to do so. They did not see the need for more classical kata in their life time because there was an abundance of them and they knew that it would take many life times to perfect just a few of them.

By the time of the 21st century however, many have enquired in the karate world on how these kata were created, if they could be, was it necessary to create more, and how it was done, just to ask a few questions. With a new idea on training by developing one's own techniques, and utilizing the rules of Kasai in a different order, these questions cannot only be answered, but any individual can create their own classical kata fighting system. They do not need to be basic. They can be whatever the creator wants them to be.

When I made the decision to start my own style of karate entitled "Nahashu Ryu" (Way of the Dominating Fist), I knew that it had to stand on the foundation of traditional karate from the past, have its own methods of training and philosophy, and capture the essence of both Naha Te (Goju Ryu), and Shuri Te (Shorin Ryu) karate as its name implies. In designing the many exercises and drills to help my students perform and learn the kata I had chosen from Naha and Shuri, I realized that I would need to create two new kata of my own that demonstrated the different styles of Naha and Shuri. Thus I created kata "Nahashu", a Naha city style kata that demonstrates the breathing techniques, circular motions, and the hard/soft powerful ways of Goju Ryu; and kata "Shuri" a Shuri city style kata that demonstrates the linear movement, speed, and power of Shorin Ryu karate. With these two kata, my style was completed. It is with the Kata "Nahashu", that I will demonstrate how to create your own Kata. Earlier I mentioned using a well known Kata from the past to check my rules against its creation. However, I believe that the reader might do this on their own to reinforce my ideas here.

Using the Rules of Kasai, but rearranging them with the addition of a few common sense rules, we will now follow it step by step through to the end and see if we get a complete kata.

Kata Nahashu Rough Draft

1. Design techniques that when used, are workable against one or more types of human aggression, and will encompass the three main rules that make them effective: close the distance, unbalance the opponent, and totally devastate them.
2. Using a partner, develop your chosen techniques so that they can be utilized as individual or connected techniques. Do not ignore turning in any direction, or the use of stances for height, or unbalancing your opponent.
3. Make sure all techniques exploit more then one of your opponent's vital areas.
4. Decide the order and placement of your techniques by which way they flow the best from one to another.
5. Remember to design techniques to show use on both the left and right side of the body.
6. If you design a technique with many applications, consider repeating it within your kata several times.
7. Any technique that you designed that moves forward to unbalance your opponent is considered offensive. Any technique moving backwards to unbalance an opponent implies defense but is still devastating.
8. Design your performance line (embusen) with space in mind. Most classical kata end where they began.

9. The line of performance can utilize all compass directions. Remember balance.
10. A hand in the chamber has something in it. If any of your techniques require pulling an opponent consider showing this by just having the pulling hand in the chambered position.
11. Touching yourself designates touching or holding a body part of your opponent. In performance of techniques, classical kata show the holding of another's body part by touching oneself near the area where the technique is performed. (An elbow smash into your own hand could mean that your opponent's head is between your hand and elbow smash.
12. Kata are performed alone.
13. Not all of your techniques are easily shown without a partner. Classical kata demonstrate pulling an opponent by the chambering of a hand or the application to a specific body part of a opponent by touching yourself in the area of that application.
14. Consider a rhythm for your kata. Breathing and changes in speed should be used to demonstrate hard and soft techniques or more complicated ones.
15. Each technique performed in your kata should be executed as if you are really doing it to an opponent in a real life situation.
16. Ways of demonstrating and remembering certain techniques must be utilized.
17. Kata exists as a way to remember your personal fighting system.
18. Pre-emptive techniques should not be neglected.

Listed numerically above is the order that I suggest to start to build and create your own kata. I will now take you step by step through the process in which I created the kata Nahashu. All of the numbers listed will correspond to the numbers listed above. I will then list the performance of the kata Nahashu and show some pictures of some of the techniques within the kata.

1. What techniques do I have that resemble Naha Te, whether created by myself or taken from the methods of Naha that can close the distance, unbalance my opponent, and totally devastate him? This is the hardest part in developing your own kata. Especially if you wish to reflect another style effectively while making it your own. It took weeks to develop techniques and borrow others that could handle multiple attack scenarios and that I really felt comfortable with. A lot were thrown out and a lot were kept because I didn't want to let them go. Finally, I decided that I would choose which techniques I would use based on several things. *These criteria would be: My likeability of a technique, it's closeness to the core traditional style of Naha Te, and a minimum of three different self defense applications that it could be used for.* Without forming these criteria, I realized that I would end up with every technique I know involved in one kata, and that it would be the world's longest kata. By limiting myself, I had plenty of left over techniques to form other kata. Since this kata was going to be the namesake of my style, I chose slowly and as wisely as I could.

2. In choosing the various techniques that I really liked and would be representative of Naha Te karate, I utilized my senior student to work with as a partner. We explored as many ways that each technique would work effectively considering as many variants as possible. Making sure to explore all angles and methods of defense that each technique could be counted on for maximum effect, we worked together to make sure that the techniques not only worked, but that we chose the best angle and scenario to use the technique within the kata.

3. By utilizing each technique to its maximum effect (not excluding likeability), I made sure that I could strike several of an opponent's vital areas at the end of the technique. Thus giving several options for the defender and making the technique of maximum benefit.

4. Once I had what I considered enough techniques that were workable to me and that I would use to defend myself, I then started to string them together to make a form. Here I considered the flow of each technique one from another as well as the possibility that two connected techniques could be utilized in conjunction with each other. Not all techniques within the kata are usable in this way but some definitely are.

5. Remembering the form of many traditional kata, I decided to utilize some techniques on the right and left side showing and reminding the practitioner that most all techniques can be executed with both the right and left side of your body. Also, that the weaker side of the body must be trained as well.

6. A few of the techniques that I decided to utilize in kata Nahashu were repeated several times because of the many known and discovered applications in them that I especially like to use.
7. By natural performance of my chosen techniques, offense is demonstrated by forward movement and defense by backward movement.
8. By this time in the process, I had to decide an embusen (performance) line. Here I let the techniques order of usage help to determine this. The starting point was easy. Flow and repetition of certain techniques dictated changes in direction. My embusen finally worked best in an upside down "T" form with the beginning in the middle of the "T's " crossbar towards Shomon like this: $+$
9. By moving left to right and front to back the kata felt balanced and could be performed in little space by manipulating the size of the movements.
10. Any chambered hand has some attacker's body part in it.
11. In no part of my kata do I touch myself.
12. Kata Nahashu, like all traditional kata is performed alone.
13. Most of the applications within kata Nahashu can be worked out in the learned observers mind. A partner attacking you in various ways for each technique would be a better way to figure out their usage. You will probably come up with your own.
14. There are obvious rhythm changes of speed within the kata. Breathing as in Sanchin is important in the first few techniques and then normal throughout. There is one transition point where the kata stops and then restarts.

15. The performance of Nahashu should indicate that there is someone in front of you as an aggressor.
16. Utilize a partner to start your own reverse engineering process.
17. This kata, performed and studied correctly helps me and my students remember their fighting system from the Naha Te side of Nahashu Ryu Karate Do.
18. All scenarios for applications should be considered including pre-emptive striking.

From each of the numbered directions above you can see how I closely followed my idea of changing the Rules of Kasai around in order to work it best to help create a Classical kata of my own. It is important that you study each part of this chapter carefully so that you understand my reasoning and how I came about my knowledge of creating a classical kata. Again, this is my idea of how they created kata hundreds of years ago and how Miyagi and Nagamine were able to create basic kata for the Okinawa school system in the 1940's. I'm not claiming any originality here, I'm just imparting something that I discovered through the rules of Kasai and my observations over 30 years of training. If what I write can help any karateka, then my mission is successful. If my writing opens doors for more knowledge and better understanding, then once again it is successful.

The Continuous Circle

I will now write the directions for the kata Nahashu as created and taught by me to all students of Nahashu Ryu Karate Do.

Kata Nahashu

1. Assume attention and loudly announce the name of the kata.
2. Assume "yoi" position.
3. From the "yoi" position with the left palm over the right and your feet in Masubi dachi, step the left foot out into hachiji dachi while placing both forearms one on top of the other, left over right palms down, in front of your chest. Breathe in deeply as this is done staying relaxed.
4. While slowly exhaling, extend both arms straight out to the sides, shoulder level, palms facing down.
5. Step into magi sanchin dachi and execute a morote chudan yoko uke while inhaling as you do and exhaling as you finish.
6. From this position inhale deeply as you pull your left hand to the chamber while leaving the right hand in the blocking position. Exhale quickly and forcefully as you execute a left chudan seiken gyaku tsuki while simultaneously returning the right hand to the chamber.
7. Immediately perform a chudan nidan tsuki leaving the left hand extended.

8. Step forward into left sanchin dachi and perform a left chudan yoko uke while inhaling deeply.
9. Exhale sharply while executing a right chudan seiken tsuki and returning the left hand to the chamber.
10. Immediately execute a chudan nidan seiken tsuki leaving the right hand extended.
11. Look to the right and turn to the right into right sanchin dachi while performing a left jodan yoko shotei uke as you do so and immediately follow with a right jodan age uke pulling the left hand to the chamber with normal breathing.
12. Step into left zenkutsu dachi and perform a left chudan nukite tsuki to the solar plexus with a loud kiai.
13. Step the left foot straight back and through heisoko dachi continuing in a straight line and finishing in shiko dachi. While doing this execute a right gedan shotei harai uke palm facing mostly outward. The left hand is open palm up in the chamber. Normal breathing. Movements 11, 12, and 13 are done very quickly with normal breathing.
14. Look to the left and step up with the right foot into left sanchin dachi while executing a right jodan yoko shotei uke followed with a left jodan age uke returning the right hand to chamber.
15. Step into right zenkutsu dachi and execute a right chudan nukite tsuki to the solar plexus with a loud kiai.
16. Step the right foot straight back and through heisoko dachi continuing in a straight line and finishing in shiko dachi. While doing this execute a left gedan shotei harai uke with the palm facing mostly outward. The right hand is in the chamber

palm up. Normal breathing. Movements 14, 15, and 16 are done very quickly with normal breathing.

17. Looking to the front, step into left sanchin dachi and execute a left kake te and a left hiki uke immediately. The right hand remains open in the chamber.

18. Perform migi kentiki geri and land in migi shiko dachi, body facing to your left and head looking forward to the front. Execute a migi hiji ate solar plexus level as your right foot hits the floor. The left hand is placed in front of your solar plexus open fingers pointing upward. Kiai loudly.

19. Perform migi uraken uchi, migi gedan uke, and step the right foot back through heisoko dachi and continuing into left foot shiko dachi, body facing to your right and head looking forward. Simultaneously perform a left gedan tetsui uchi with the right hand chambered.

20. Looking to the back, step the left foot up into right sanchin dachi and perform a right chudan kake te and a right hiki uke immediately. The left hand is open in the chamber.

21. Perform hidari kentiki geri and land in hidari shiko dachi body facing to your right and head looking to the back opposite shomon. Execute an open hand hidari hiji ate chudan level when the left foot hits the floor. The open right hand is placed in front of your solar plexus fingers pointing up. Kiai loudly.

22. Perform hidari uraken uchi, hidari gedan uke, and step the left foot straight back and through heisoko dachi continuing into right shiko dachi, body facing your left and head looking toward the back still opposite shomon. Perform a right gedan tetsui uchi with your left hand chambered.

23. Turn your head and look to the front (shomon). Step your left foot towards the left ending up in hidari zenkutsu dachi while executing a hidari jodan yoko tetsui uchi and a migi chudan seiken gyaku tsuki. This is the transition place in the kata. A short pause is taken here to emphasize a change.

24. Step the left foot back through heisoko dachi and ending in a right foot shiko dachi with your body facing your left but your head looking forward to the front. Simultaneously perform hari uke with open hands – right gedan barai and an open hand left jodan age uke, performed together. Inhale deeply while moving your body into position and exhale long and slowly while finishing the techniques. This movement should be done slowly and gracefully.

25. Same as #24 above but start by moving the right foot back into left shiko dachi.

26. Step the right foot forward through heisoku dachi and ending in right foot shiko dachi with your body facing your left and head forward, perform a right open hand jodan age uke and at the same time placing the left open hand palm up just under the right pectoral muscle. This movement resembles a right open hand hiji ate with the left arm resting in front of chudan. This technique is also peformed with slow deep breathing in and out.

27. Very quickly slide (suri ashi) the right foot back while performing a right ura uke. Immediately slide (suri ashi) forward and perform a morote tsuki left hand on top and kiai very loudly.

28. As quickly as you can, transition from #27 step back into left foot neko ashi dachi performing a left tora guchi (circular block).

29. Now slowly step back into right foot neko ashi dachi and perform a right tora guchi inhaling long and deep while preparing the technique and exhaling long and slow while executing the technique.
30. Move your left hand down to meet your right hand and while stepping back into masubi dachi raise your hands up and over and down to the "yoi" position. Place both hands by your sides in attention stance.
31. Bow.

As the creator of this kata I tried to be as precise as possible in my directions. At times I used the Japanese language to better describe techniques. I always try to teach techniques to my classes in Japanese so that if they are in front of a Japanese high ranking person for instruction, they will understand better. This helps with diplomacy and it is always useful to engage ourselves in learning others' languages. There is an appendix at the end of this book on some Japanese terminology for those of you who need the help. I chose not to show a series of pictures with the written directions since I believe the description is well enough explained and makes you think more and be more careful in the movements described. Following are just a few pictures of some of the techniques within the kata Nahashu as performed by one of my senior black belt students. They are not in any specific order and I have not included any of my applications to the techniques I used in the kata that were either my own, or techniques widely known from other Naha kata.

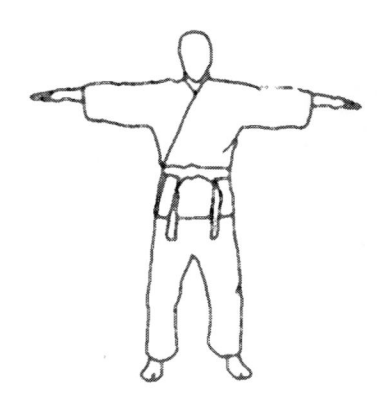

If you put this kata together from my written directions, then you should be able to find your own techniques. Will you stumble on some of the techniques that I use in my fighting system? You probably will, but you will never know it unless we meet at a seminar or you train with some of my students who know the Nahashu Ryu Karate Do fighting system. Thus you can see that you are stuck in your knowledge of what is the correct or right technique that I, the creator use. Just like all of us are continually trying to guess the correct technique that the creators of the classical kata from the past were trying to do. It brings us back to the same problem that we have had from the beginning of this book. No one knows because the records were not kept or passed down correctly. Additionally, the authors of the classical kata are all dead. Does it really all matter though?

The answer is yes; why? Because by laying my ideas out on paper on how kata were created I have come full circle in karate. This venture has rewarded me immensely. There is so much that I've learned through this process. It all may seem too simple to many of you out there. Sometimes though, it is right under our noses and we don't see it. Then the light goes on and we are almost ashamed of ourselves for not seeing it earlier. In that respect this book had to be written. Sometimes all we need is the organization of information from others who came before us (sensei) to push us or to get us motivated to utilize what we already know in an orderly fashion.

If you haven't read the Introduction to this book, then you have missed the whole idea behind it. It is my sincerest hope that you have found something within these pages that is useful to you.

Train hard, train often.

Peace.

NOTES

APPENDIX A

Japanese Terminology

The terminology written here is a general knowledge of the terms written within this book.

Stances

Heisoku Dachi……….Feet together

Masubi Dachi………..Attention Stance

Heiko Dachi………….Shoulder width stance

Zen Kutsu Dachi……..Front Stance

Shiko Dachi………….Sumo Stance

Sanchin Dachi………..Hour Glass stance

Neko Ashi Dachi……..Cat foot stance

Strikes

Jodan Tsuki……….Upper punch

Chudan Tsuki……..Middle punch

Gedan Tsuke………Lower punch

Nukite Tsuki………Finger thrust

Hiji Ate……………Elbow smash

Uraken Uchi……….Back fist strike

Yoko Tetsui Uchi..Side hammerfist

Awase Tsuki……..Double punch

Blocks

Morote Chudan Uke…….Double middle block

Jodan Yoko Shotei………Upper palm heel block

Jodan Age Uke………….Upper rising block

Otoshi Shotei Uke………Downward Palm Heel Block

Hike te……………,…..Grasping Block

Kicks

Mae Geri……………Front Kick

Kake te......................Hooking Block

Gedan Barai................Lower Sweeping Block

Hari Uke....................Bow and Arrow Block

Tora Guchi.................Tiger Mouth Block (circular block)

Ura Kake Uke..............Back – Hand Hook Block

General Vocabulary

Yoi............Ready

Kyotsuki.....Attention

Rei............Bow

Yame.........Finish

Sensei........Teacher/One who came before

Dojo..........Place to train "The Way"

Migi,,,,,,,,,,,Right

Hidari.........Left

Appendix B

Recommended Reading and Viewing

BOOKS

By Iain Abernethy

Bunkai Jutsu
Armlocks for all Styles
Throws for Strikers
Karate's Grappling Methods

By Bill Burgar

Five Years, One Kata

By Lawrence Kane and Kris Wilder

The Way of Kata

By Shoshin Nagamine

Okinawan Karate Do

By Patrick McCarthy

Ancient Okinawan Martial Arts; Koryu Uchinade Vol. 2

By Seikichi Toguchi

Okinawan Goju Ryu II, Advanced Techniques of Shorei-Kan Karate

DVD'S

By Iain Abernethy

Bukai Jutsu Volumes 1 – 6

Bibliography

1. Abernethy, Iain; Bunkai Jutsu, The Practical Applications of Karate Kata, Neth Publishing, UK © Copyright 2002
2. Burgar, Bill, Five Years, One Kata, Martial Arts Publishing Limited, UK © Copyright 2003
3. Kane, Lawrence A. & Wilder, Kris; The Way of Kata, A Comprehensive Guide to Deciphering Martial Applications, YMAA Publications © Copyright 2005
4. Nagamine, Shoshin, The Essence of Okinawan Karate-Do, Charles E. Tuttle Co., Inc. © Copyright 1976
5. McCarthy, Patrick, Ancient Okinawan Martial Arts Vol. 2, Koryu Uchinadi, Tuttle Publishing, © Copyright 1999
6. Toguchi, Seikichi, Okinawan Goju Ryu II, Advanced Techniques of Shorei-Kan Karate, Ohara Publications, Inc. © Copyright 2001

About the Author

Soke Dave Nielsen, Hanshi, JuDan (10th Degree Black Belt), is the chief instructor and founder of the Nahashu Ryu Karate-Do system. He is also the founder of the United States of America Traditional Karate Association (USATKA), which has members of various traditional karate styles in the United States.

His martial arts experience spans three decades where he began in Goju Ryu and continued on to the style of Shito Ryu before forming his style of Nahashu Ryu in 2003. Accepting only the rank of a Fifth Degree Black Belt, he began to meticulously hone the physical, mental, and spiritual aspects of his own style while studying the birth of modern karate through the original style of its predecessor, Okinawan Tuite. Through the study of Reverse Engineering and building upon the findings of such martial artists as Patrick McCarthy, Iain Abernethy, and Bill Burgar, Soke Nielsen has stepped out and put into writing the first material on how the karate masters from the past must have created their own kata. Not just their fighting system, but the actual way in which they remembered it and how they grouped their techniques together. Now in print for readers of all styles of the martial arts to study, scrutinize and enjoy, Soke Nielsen hopes to increase the awareness of kata, and why modern students should not be discouraged to create their own. Herein lays the blueprint in order to do just that.

Accepting the rank of 10th Degree Black Belt and the title of Hanshi in June of 2008, Soke Nielsen continues to write and spread his style throughout the United States and abroad. He is available for seminars and can be contacted by emailing him at usatka@hotmail.com. His hope is that this book will be built upon with ever growing knowledge and better ideas than his own by other practitioners of traditional styles of karate.

Printed in Great Britain
by Amazon.co.uk, Ltd.,
Marston Gate.